W9-BOM-107

Introduction

Through the stories I tell in this book, I hope to lead my readers on their own personal journey to discover Jesus as He reveals himself in the ordinary experiences of daily life as well as in particular Scriptural episodes. The outcome for them would ideally be an encounter with Jesus, in a spirit of freedom, as someone who is still speaking and acting in our present world, rather than as a voice from two thousand years ago that has nothing new to say to us today.

The stories do not draw conclusions for the readers, but lead them to ask their own questions and draw their own conclusions.

Foreword

Father Frascadore's delightful book reminds us of the oneness with nature we felt as children. He shares the wisdom to be gained at Hector's Market, at grandpa's knee, and at the end of Ramsey's leash. Most rewarding, I think, are his poetic insights into the mind of Christ. There is poetry in the New Testament, but nothing like the lushness of 150 psalms. Perhaps God is inviting us to compose our own psalters. Father Frascadore has accepted the invitation and shown us what can be done.

~~~~~ Reverend Henry P. Cody

Table of Contents

A Shepherd

how lucky we are to have a shepherd
    to walk with each evening
        in pastures that are green
where we pause for a while
    to rest by running waters
        to review the day
we go over the things that we've done
    the people we've met
        and the thoughts we've had
he is easy to talk to
    and the evening passes gently
        we're relaxed
and if at times
    we get confused about the things
        we're doing
and begin to wonder
    which paths
        to take
he gently takes our hand
    and sets us in a direction
        we know will be a better way
even though we have questions
    and no ready answers
        we are not afraid
his presence
    calms us
        and our steps grow confident
as the day closes
    we approach a cottage
        set on a hillside
it's one that we have
    been to before
        we recognize the flower beds
the tall tree that
    stands straight behind it
        and the light in the window
the table inside
    is set with
        delectable things

there's fruit in a bowl
   roast lamb on a platter
     and bread in a straw basket
we think
   how lucky we've been
     to know someone like him
our lives are full
   more than full
     they are overflowing
let them spill
   for what do we have to fear
     we trust that his goodness
will follow us
   all the days of our lives
     yes, everlastingly

A Woman's Point of View

Jesus was fortunate
to have a group of women,
among them Mary and Joanna and Susanna,
following him and his disciples
as they went through Palestine
proclaiming the good news of the Kingdom.

At night
he would hear
different points of view
on the day's happenings.

Certainly the loneliness of the ten lepers,
separated from their wives and children,
must have been the subject
of a conversation,

and how the old people
dealt with the long journey to Tabor,
as well as the young woman caught in adultery,

and how Jairus and his wife reacted when they saw their daughter
get up from her death bed
and run to her friends,

and the feelings
each had
when Jesus said that Jerusalem
would be the end of his journey.

There is no doubt
that the men and women
in his band of followers
looked at things differently.

And Jesus listened confidently
to all that was said
knowing that wisdom
is a community's gift.

Balthazar

balthazar grew up staring at the stars
he was a stargazer by birth
it was in his blood
his father was a stargazer
from him he learned the names of the stars
where they were set in the sky
when they came out and went in
but this night a particular star troubled him
he hadn't seen it before
it was the brightest he had ever seen
 and it was moving
he told his two friends that it
forecast the birth of a king

they packed their bags and headed west
across the desert and through the mountains
until they reached the tiny town
of bethlehem entered a barn behind a crowded inn
and fell on their knees
before a young girl holding a baby in her arms
it wasn't the kind of place
or the kind of king
they had expected to find
cows sheep trough and three people in poor clothes
balthazar looked beyond all that to the face of the child
and saw there the world's desire for meaning
it would be his longest moment
and wondered if that moment would ever end
he asked the child's name
the man standing by the girl said
Jesus
having seen what they had come to see
they laid their gifts
of gold, incense and myrrh
at the foot of the manger
bowed and returned home
the journey was finished for his friends

but not for balthazar
the face and name of Jesus went with him
never again could he look at the stars without hoping
to see once more a brilliant star that moved
signaling that the child had grown and had taken
his place upon a throne
more than thirty years passed and a star rose
 brilliant and moving just the same alone this time balthazar
followed it to bethlehem
and there asked if they knew where Jesus the king could be found
some smiled others said the Jesus
 who says he's a king
can be found in jerusalem
balthazar headed that way immediately

and when he got to the city
he asked of a screaming crowd
where is Jesus
they pointed to the top of a hill
he climbed it as fast as he could
and got there just as they laid
the beaten, torn body of Jesus
in the arms of his mother
balthazar knelt by her side
took from a small bag that he had
tied to his belt years ago
a piece of gold, a grain of incense and a bit of myrrh
and said gently to Mary
you hold again
as first I saw you
the holy king my star foretold

the hillside was covered with people who
      had walked miles to hear Jesus preach.
      it was a long day, and as evening approached, the crowd grew hungry.
      Jesus knew that the disciples hadn't brought food; nor had they money to buy any.
      Andrew, the most observant of Jesus' followers,
      spotted a boy with a bag. He asked what the boy had.
      " two fish and five loaves of bread" he said.
      Andrew brought the boy to Jesus.
      "will this be enough?" the boy asked Jesus.
      Jesus smiled, "is this all you have?"
      "yes," the boy said," it is all I have."
      "then... it is enough."
      Jesus handed the bread and fish back to the boy and told him to pass
      it on to Andrew, and to Mary, and to Phoebe and the others on the hillside.
      the crowd followed the boy's example and all had enough to eat.

Epiphany

when everyone was still asleep,
they slipped out of their homes
to study the skies.
the night was clear and
the stars brighter than
they ever were;
a perfect night for doing what stargazers do:
chart the position of the stars
hoping to discern the destinies of empires
and the fortunes of kings and queens.
this night they saw
one star much brighter than the rest
moving across the sky.
it was the moment they had lived for:
the first observers of a heavenly
sign that the world was about to change.
quickly they returned to their homes,
kissed their wives,
hugged their children,
loaded their bags on the backs of their camels
and headed west following the star
'til it stopped over a barn behind an inn
on the outside of a small forgotten town.
it wasn't what they had expected to see,
a palace is what they had in mind,
large rooms and long halls,
not a barn with oxen
and a baby in a straw-filled crib
watched over by a young girl
and a rugged man in workman's clothes.

what would they,
these three simple people,
make of gold, myrrh and of incense?
should we turn and take these gifts back with us,
or leave them here
beside the baby's bed?
"obey the stars,
is what our fathers said to do,
so we'll leave them here
where the star has stopped."

as they knelt to place the
frankincense, gold and myrrh
beside the baby's bed
they looked closely at his face
and knew at once that
their journey was not about
palaces and gifts but about
the possibilities of
a new world,
a new humanity,
a new life for all.
they could see that in the baby's eyes.

the wise ones stood, smiled and
thanked the girl and man
for the precious moments shared
and with a few words bid them farewell.
then they turned, climbed upon their camels backs
and headed east back home to their families
and the lives they were being called to live,
lives in search of the possibilities
the infant's eyes foretold:
the peace that can't be found unless it's sought,
the justice that can't be seen unless our eyes are open wide,
the mercy that can't be felt unless there's passion in our hearts.

the magi had the courage
to go in search of the unknown
and returned having found out
who they were to be.

Good Friday

arms stretched across rough, hard wood
and iron nails pounded in his hands and feet
then the cross was lifted up to display the tortuous arrival of death.
and to insure that death had come, a soldier rammed a spear
into the chest of Jesus and blood poured forth, enough red blood
to quench the thirst of all

How Much Is a Dreamer Worth?

Joseph was the eleventh of
the twelve sons of Jacob. he was a dreamer. his father liked that,
the brothers hated listening
to his dreams.
they plotted to kill him
by stuffing him in a dry well.
death without a mark on him, perhaps an accident!
but no sooner had they put joseph in the well,
when along came a caravan of Ishmaelites, of all people, driving
camels to Egypt.
 a thought popped into the brothers' heads.
"why kill him, when we can sell him?"
"how much can we get for this dreamer?"
"twenty silver pieces."
"a deal."

years later, another dreamer came along.
to make things right, he wanted to turn the
world upside down.
the people in charge of it
didn't go along with his dream,
so they bought him for
thirty pieces of silver.
the price hadn't gone up much in
thirteen hundred years!
there's never been a big market for dreamers.

It's All about Trust

Nazareth was a small hillside village in Galilee
about four hundred people lived there
most of them were olive pickers or vine tenders
they all knew Mary and Joseph
had watched them grow up
and heard their vows of love

so when Mary departed
without a word to Joseph
news traveled quickly
it fell to a neighbor to tell him
that Mary was pregnant and had left town

the world he had built with her
came apart
nothing made sense
why did she leave without a word
where had she gone
was she coming back
he was bewildered
without her time seemed endless
finally he decided to divorce her
he had the right to do that
for they had not lived together
finally Gabriel came again
this time to Joseph
he told him of Mary's yes
to the bearing of Jesus
and of Elizabeth's pregnancy
and of her need for Mary's presence

would Joseph accept this
mystery of God as Mary did
Gabriel waited
the wait for Joseph's answer
seemed as long as Mary's did
would the yes ever come and
put things back together again
it did

Mary made the long trip
back from Elizabeth's home
to Nazareth
she went immediately
to where Joseph was working
he saw her coming
got down from his ladder
and walked toward her

Mary looked lovely
he wrapped his arms around her and the baby within
no words were spoken
trust doesn't need words

Jesus Is Blunt

Jesus doesn't mince his words.
he says exactly what he means.
last night at a dinner hosted by one of the town's leading Pharisees,
i sat next to Jesus at the table.
half way through dinner, i heard him say to the host,
      to your next dinner be sure to invite
        not only the wealthy who can repay the favor
        but the poor, lame, crippled and blind who can't.
that was blunt.

Jesus told the host to face his prejudices
and to stare straight at the way he treats people.
the host stood up, said nothing, and walked away.
that was the last dinner invitation
we received from him.

Jesus always makes his point clearly.
he says what needs to be said.
i've heard him do it that way
ever since i began following him two years ago.

i was with him when he called the clerics
two-faced for asking people to do things that
they wouldn't do themselves.

and I can't forget
the look on the faces of the elders
when he invited them to throw the first stone
at the woman charged with sin
...but only if they were sinless.

his bluntness is what i like about him.
it gets him into trouble
but he knows that if he doesn't
say what's on his mind
things will go on just as they are.
and that's not what he wants.
he came to change the status quo
and to do that he had to be blunt.
it didn't bother him
and it shouldn't bother us.

Juggling Cotton Balls

Paul convinces us today
    That it would have
        Been easier to
            Juggle cotton balls
              In the wind
Than to change people's
    Lives by his words.
        He tried for three months
            To do that and failed.
So he did
    What all saints do:
        He got out of the way
            And let the Spirit
              Work through his words.
As soon as he did that
    Miracles began to happen
        And the people of Ephesus
            Accepted the words of Jesus.

So don't waste time trying to
    Juggle cotton balls in the wind.
        Get out of the way
        And let the Spirit
            Do the work.

Lazarus Risen

when a loved one dies, the whole world changes:
there is no one with whom to share the full moon;
tomorrows hold no interest;
dinner becomes an empty ritual.
Martha and Mary experienced this when Lazarus died:
        he was the one who
        told the story of Mary getting her long hair
        caught in the pricker bush
        and how he had to cut her free.
Martha and Mary thought that life would never be the same again.
they were wrong.
Jesus got word that Lazarus died and went back to Bethany.
        before a large crowd,
        Jesus shouted at the tombstone
        and Lazarus came out, full of new life.
once his sisters unwrapped his body and face,
and the ooh's and ah's quieted down
Lazarus began to speak.
        he told everyone that he hadn't wanted to come back,
        that he liked it where he was,
        it was more beautiful than he had imagined,
but Jesus wanted him, so he came.
quickly life at Bethany returned to normal.
it was as though nothing had happened.
when Martha and Mary heard that Jesus and his disciples were returning
they planned a party.
Mary would cook her favorite dinner:
roast lamb over an open fire pit;
and Mary, as though she knew what lay ahead,
would plan an anointing.

the guests enjoyed the lamb,
        Judas objected to the waste of precious perfume,
        and Jesus told him that there was more to life than money.
Lazarus thanked Jesus for another chance at life.
        "if I have learned anything," he said,
        "it is to applaud every moment I am given."
the crowd heard what he had to say and
marveled at the disciples' stories,
had another glass of wine,
and a second helping of lamb.

Lazarus

with a wire
razor sharp,
a potter frees his pot
from the wheel and
prepares it for firing,
the final stage of his art.

Jesus stands before
the sealed tomb of his friend,
and says,
"take the stone away."
Then He shouts,
"Lazarus, come out."
bound head to foot
in linen cloths,
Lazarus stands before
those who love him.

then Jesus says,
"untie him,
sever the bonds,
let him go"
today Lazarus stands for us.
come out of the darkness,

Jesus shouts
stand in the sunlight,
untie the straps
that hold you,
to what you were
and become now
what you
have always hoped
to be: fully alive,
fully alive to the
life you have been given to live.
sever the cords that
bind you to addictions
sever the relationships
that fool you into
believing that they
make life meaningful
cut the reins
that pull the fantasies
of beauty, wealth,
power and control,
pause before
a mirror that doesn't lie,
slash the ropes
that tied you
to poles of self-doubt
and begin to say
what you need to say
not what you ought to say
finally do what brings you happiness
rather than bow to
the comfort of routine.

as the pot is freed
from the potter's wheel
by the deft motion of
the potter's wire,
so too, can you be freed
to be what in your
silent moments
you hoped to be.
within the clay of
each of us
there is a work of art
waiting to be called forth
by the divine potter
who knows us
as we truly are.
come forth, He shouts.
come forth.
live to the fullest moment.
you are in.
you are alive now.
rejoice and be glad.

Reach Beyond Our Reach

why do we waste our time
reaching for what we cannot grasp
we try time and time again
to write exactly what we mean to say
to draw the loveliest profile
to compose the finest melody
        and we fail to be the greatest
but we keep on trying
for our happiness
is found in the reaching

kings don't like rabble-rousers
john was one
the king had him arrested
and then who knows what happened

when Jesus heard about it
he left nazareth and went north
to capernaum
where some say he had a home
whether he did or not is beside the point
it was a place that he liked
a lot of memories were made there
his first disciples and the night sounds of the sea
as often happens plans for thought and rest get interrupted
word got out fast that he was in galilee and people from
as far away as syria judea jerusalem and decapolis
came bringing with them the blind and crippled
paralytics and lunatics
all for curing by the hands of Jesus

if Jesus learned anything from the sea
it was that changes come suddenly
and interruptions like these were
to be accepted

as much as he had dreamed of a retreat
to get his life back together
it wasn't going to happen this time
perhaps the next

Noah

Noah was in his garden tending
to the cabbage, leeks and garlic
when God interrupted him and told him
to put down the hoe and pick up the saw
for he had an ark to build
what the Lord said was
> go to the hills and cut and haul down as many
> gopher trees as you can find and
> follow the blueprints i give you.
> i am not happy with the
> way my people are acting.

Noah sawed and hammered
the pieces together
the neighbors wondered why a gardener was
building an ark in his back yard
they passed it off as a mid-life crisis
that is until the bow rose higher
than a sycamore tree and the hull filled the field behind Noah's house
then they began to panic
what did Noah know that they didn't
they got their answer when raindrops
as big as figs began to bounce off the roof tops
and tables floated down main street
the Lord told Noah to take aboard what was important
his wife and three sons with their wives

and two of every animal he could get his hands on
forty days and forty nights later
when the dove returned with
an olive branch in its beak
Noah knew it was time to disembark
he lowered the gang plank to solid ground
and told his passengers we've had plenty
of time to review our lives, correct our mistakes
and now we have another chance to begin
let's do it right this time

today Jesus reviews for his disciples
a bit of their history.
he says
     remember Noah
     and what happened to the
     people who had forgotten
     about God, and believed that they
     had all the time in the world
     to do as they pleased
     so stay awake
     raindrops as big as figs
     are in the forecast
     build an ark for yourselves
     and bring on board
     the four sayings of mine that arouse your spirits
     the three people who make a
     difference in your life
     the two things you can't live without
     the one dream you have yet to live,
     the person you want by your side at life's end

then Jesus added
     the waters will recede
     and you'll begin life on solid ground again
     it's a second chance to do things differently
     if you're not happy with
     the way they've gone so far
the sun broke through the clouds
the waves flattened out
and a dove perched on the bow
land is near
he continued
     hold fast to what matters most
     for that is all that matters

A Companion at Seven

when we were seven we had a companion
that walked with us
wherever we went
we had no name for him
he never introduced himself
he just tagged along
at hammonasset beach
and on the hike to tory's den
and to the world's fair in new york

i don't think that it
was fair of him
to put questions in our heads
that we had no words for
did the pebbles feel it when
we walked on them
does the ocean
hear its own voice
are roses aware
of their intricacies
can the trees hear us
how does a flock of swallows
know when to land
all at once
on the same bush

our companion
had a plan in mind
for us
he put all of these questions
in our minds when
we were young
hoping that as we grew
we'd spend the rest
of our lives looking for the words
to describe our
provocative friendship
with curiosity

A Man in the Park

Early in the morning,
I often pass a man walking in Bushnell Park.
He looks like a poor man,
the way he's dressed,
old pants and ragged jacket.
He walks with a limp
and carries a cane.
He looks like a poor man,
teeth that are brown and haven't been cared for,
beaten up shoes, and now that it is cold,
a sad looking ski cap.
He looks poor,
but that's a guess.
I saw him the other day
sitting alone on a metal bench by the Lily Pond and talking to the fish.
and I assumed wildly that
he was telling them
the things that caught his eye that morning
on his walk:
the profile of the Travelers' building
against the morning sky,
the Turkey oak tree that's been in the park
for a hundred and fifty years,
and dogs staying in shape
by chasing tennis balls.
If that's the case
the fish would know him as richer
than ...I thought he was.

A Note in a Wheelbarrow

i was a junior in high school
when the music director
told me that i couldn't
carry a note in a wheelbarrow
that was a heck of a thing
to say to a kid
who was planning to spend
his life singing God's praises
some sentences stay with us
all through life
his sentence has stayed with me
i think of it
every Sunday
when i am asked
to join my voice with
the angels
who have been singing
God's praises
forever
if i am good enough to sing
with such a heavenly choir
who was he to keep
me from singing with
a bunch of boys who were
far more interested in learning
to shoot a foul shot
than sing gregorian chant
i think back to his words
every sunday when before hundreds
of faithful people i chant with the spirit
the ultimate mystery of faith

and another thing
to add insult to injury
he told me in my first year of college
that he wouldn't let me into the schola cantorum
even if i had the voice of enrico caruso
fortunately i am a resilient chap
so bravely week after week
i sing out like rushing water
like ringing bells
and like a harp strummed by
angelic fingers
so there

A Sentence Never Forgotten

on august 26th, 1956
my grandfather said something to me
that i won't forget

he was in a hospital bed
and it was the last time
i saw him alive

but before i tell you what he said
here's a sketch
of who he was.

a faithful Presbyterian
beginning each day reading scripture
and ending it the same way

never sitting at the table
to eat without bowing
his head in prayer

I have his bible
on a table near my desk
to remind me of him

he was a hunter
fisherman lover of animals
and a farmer of sorts

i also have a silver watch of his
which he carried in a little pocket
in his woolen pants

why he had a watch
i don't know
he never seemed to be in a hurry

he followed a daily routine
feed the chickens rabbits goats and
his two pekinese dogs maisie and teddy

and his words
that i will
never forget

i was standing close to his bedside
he stretched out his hand
and said simply
i am going to the father and
i will be waiting
for you when you come

those words
have affected
 my life ever since

heaven
is not an idea
i struggle to define

it is where my grandfather
is waiting for me
to arrive

he will be the same
person i remember teaching me
to gather eggs from the chicken coop

put a worm on a hook
saw a piece of wood
row a boat shoot a b-b gun

he will still be wearing his woolen cap
lighting his pipe with blue tip matches
and building lawn chairs

heaven is the everlasting home
where we will live with
those we know and love

it is the home
the father has prepared for his children.

A Walk in the Woods

There is no such thing
as a quiet walk in the woods
in early November
after the leaves of every tree
have fallen on the trail
and persist in crunching under every step I take.
They say the Indians
could walk through the woods
and silently surprise a deer.
I believe it
but it is hard to imagine that
listening to the noise
I am making.
But they had been taught since birth
to reverence the earth,
the mother that gave them
wheat and flowers and running water.
She was to be treated
with respect,
with great care,
and listened to for what
the wind had to say
of a bear's rising,
or a boulder 's story about
the midnight feel of a full moon.
They had to walk in silence,
like a monk
in prayer,
listening and never speaking
for divinity was all around them
even in the
deep scarlet leaves on a
tiny berry bush
off to the right of the trail,
on my way back home.

A Winter's Morning at 5:45

how beautiful the words of the psalms at this time of day
how satisfying the first cup of coffee
i delight in
the muffled sound of traffic from the street below my window
the first look out over the city at its awakening
the first apartment lights being turned on
the shine of the capitol's golden dome
the street lights and headlights
the dawn profile of the city's office buildings
i delight in
the comfortable feel of my favorite chair
the warmth of my bathrobe
the feel of my slippers
the silence of the room
the thoughts of what the day will hold
the joy of knowing that God is listening
the thoughts of my friends
the continuing search for who i will be today

i delight in
the wonder of just having the will to wonder
the questions i suspect will come up during the day
the catching of ideas
the losing of ideas
the wondering where new ideas come from
the regrets that i don't know as much as i'd like to know
the wish that i'll remember at least some of what i'll read today
the energy to keep searching for the words that say what i want them to say
i delight in
the look on ramsey's face when he wakes up
the look on his face when i pet his ears
the thought that the dog and i are the first two creatures to meet each day
and wondering if he has a film of yesterday's events running through his mind
and then i delight in (while not as much)
the thought that i have to get up and out of
my chair put on winter's clothes boots and heavy jacket and take ramsey
out into the snow so that he can renew his acquaintance with every
lamp post trash can and tree trunk in bushnell park

I Was on a Mission

I knew where I was going
as I flew by Bushnell Tower on Monday morning
a few minutes after seven.
I had a destination in mind,
a place I had been thinking about for a while;
so I flew north,
dodging the traffic light on Wells Street,
skirting an old oak tree
which I thought for sure had fallen in the last wind storm
and headed for the garden
next to the Hoadley Bridge.

Its flowers had died and their places taken
by leaves from the linden trees near it,
the same kind of tree that
I had just come from.

This is the place I had in mind;
it is where I wanted to be with my friends,
the leaves I shared so many days with
during the spring, summer and early fall.

We'd have a lot to talk about:
the crowds of kids who rode
around on the backs of painted
horses in the carousel,

retrievers running at top speed to fetch balls thrown by their owners,
visitors from Pennsylvania who came to see the Memorial Arch
and couldn't stop talking about
how little they knew of the Civil War,
and old people who sat on benches by the pond
and admired our changing colors in October.

Oh, we'd have a lot to talk about,
so I landed in the garden bed
and with my friends
settled in for a winter beneath the snow
to patiently await
the warmth of spring
and the rising of our memories
in the beauty of its flowers' faces.

Become What We Are Meant To Be

You break the darkness
And unveil the dawn,
Your silent call to begin again
The thing we left undone.
With a mighty wind
Rage on, rage on, and rattle our souls
Shake them from their dream-full sleep
To what is and what is yet to be.
Hold high your brilliant flame
That we might see new horizons
And know that they are within our reach,
If we but try as not before.
Unfasten our tongues, free them
To say needy words and not the ones
That please...for they leave us where we were
And not where we need to be.
Replace our spirit with one that's yours,
Startle us with your vision of who we are.
Then, yes then give us the courage to
Fulfill what you see.
We are much more than we think we are
But that's our fear.
We buckle in the face of trying to become what
We are meant to be.
On our own that can't be done
But with your hand it can,
So send forth your spirit
and we shall be recreated
And you through us
shall renew the face of the earth.

Bounce Back

the first lesson of the spiritual life
can be learned by watching
third graders race around the schoolyard
at recess
they run fast holler and fall
kids fall in schoolyards
it's called growing up
and the lesson they teach us is
bounce up
and start running again
maximilian kolbe in his daily journal
wrote that
...be careful not to fall;
but if you fall,
...rise again.
i suspect that he had
school children in mind
when he wrote that
Jesus tells us that heaven is filled
with children
who fell at recess and
bounced up before the
teacher had a chance to scold them

Chapman Falls: Devil's Hop Yard

I have heard
people say
 "listen to the water
falling on the rocks."
and wonder what they hear.

I have heard people say,
"see the mist that rises
when the water falls"
and wonder what they see.

I have caught the scent
of falling waters
and have no idea
from where it comes.

"Why me? Why have you
held from me
the marvel of the falls
and the cause
for its wet touch
upon my face when
I stand close by?"

Perhaps you have waited
until now
to open up my eyes
that when I see it fall
the expression in my eyes
will awaken those
who take no note of it all!

Everlasting Love

a cherry coke at the counter
of my father's grocery store
the feel of my mom's hand holding mine
while crossing terryville avenue
the late night antics of my brother
in the cot next to mine in the tent by the shore
are among the first memories
i have of my life
In the seventy or so years
since those early times
i've lived a thousand
      more memories
of people i've met, things that i've done
and places i've been
and all in the light
      of this truth
that God's love for me is as great today
as it was way back then
when i sat at the counter
crossed the avenue and slept in a cot by the shore
and so it will be
forever more

Frank Woolever

our lives are
     the sum of the
          lives we have shared.
we are:
     composites,
          tapestries,
               melodies,
put together,
     woven,
          arranged,
through
     the years
          by the
people,
     friends
          and loves
which have
     filled
          our days and years.
when others
     ask
          who we are,
we answer
     as best
          we can:
we are
     who we are
          in relation
to the memories
     we possess
          at the moment.
right now
     i am the sum
          of the memories of Frank
of our years
     at Rochester,
          our walks and talks,

our games of handball,
     our ordinations,
          our vacations,
the questions we asked,
     the answers we gave,
          the people we met,
the kind of love
     that
          changed lives.
and the love
     that makes
          of two one.
at this moment
     i am the sum of my
          memories of Frank
a marvelous friend
     who did the most
          marvelous thing:
               lived what he believed.

never put your finger on the scale
is one of the important things i learned as a kid
at hector's market, my father's grocery store
a pound of hamburger, he told me, should be sixteen ounces
of beef not fourteen and two ounces of thumb
Jesus says today
for the measure you measure with
will in return be measured out to you
how lucky i was that i had a father
who agreed with Jesus.

Little Things in Us Make Us Big

there are billions
of little atoms
in all of us when we die
since time began
some of them
have passed through
jupiter and mars
ursa major everest
and little things like fleas
some in us
have spent time
in alexander joan mozart
and other people with famous names
there's a little bit
of everything and everyone
in everyone of us
so when paul said
we are unique
he was far ahead
of the scientists and geneticists
holiness breaks
like dawn
when we realize
      just how special we are

Live Your Life Out Loud

the teacher told me
to shout my life out loud.
he didn't tell me
how to do it.
that was left to me.
so i decided to live
my life as an orchestra,
the liveliest
orchestra of all time
with piano,
trumpets, drums
and strings.
i became popular
playing the kind
of music
that moved people from their chairs
to the floor
for the happiest
dance of their lives.
i saw the teacher smile when
he passed by my room
and watched the dancers
in full swing.
he called me over and said,
" when i told you
to live your
life out loud,
i never thought you'd be an orchestra.
but you went for it
and did well.
that's all that matters."

Love and Hate

how can we hate our life
when we have been given so much
and know that so much is still
to be given?

hate happens when we realize
that we cannot hold onto life
long enough to continue its receiving
and our waiting for its giving.

in the end, hate releases its grip
to love and finds the giving and receiving
of life goes on forever.

The First Snow in the Park

the park benches
    are empty
the fountains in the pond
    are shut down
the carousel
    is silent
the trees are
    nearly bare
the sidewalks
    are stamped with fallen leaves
the city's buildings stand clear
    against dawn's granite sky
winter is very near
    leaving us only to remember
buds on empty branches
    anxious to get on with life
green houses suspended in mid-air
    occupied by squirrels and birds
boulevards of beautiful faces
    one more beautiful than the next
and the precious thought that what is ending
    is already preparing to begin again
it is not by chance that a
    white canvas
has been stretched
    across the whole park
to challenge the artist within us
    to try again to recapture
the original masterpiece

Rembrandt's Memoirs

They asked me to
write my memoirs.
I told them to look
at my self-portraits instead.
The features of my face,
which I have painted many times
during my life, will tell
you more about me
than I could ever put in a book.
I started these portraits,
these journals, as I call them,
when I was very young,
and have kept up with them
through these past sixty years.
My features
tell you the story of my life.
Look carefully at the changing
shape of my face,
the line of my jaw,
and the gradual darkening of my eyes,
you'll see there the struggles I have had
with the fickleness of fame,
the envy of my friends,
and the loss of my greatest love.
Oh, yes, it is all there.
And I found the same kind of stories
in the features of the people who
have sat for me.

I got beyond
their profile and saw what was
going on in their souls,
just as I did with myself,
and in some way
made them immortal.
So when you look
at the paintings I've done of
people like James
or the boy in the street
you'll come away thinking that
they're leaving the canvas
and walking along beside you;
you'll feel you know them inside and out.
And being able to do that for you,
with a brush and paint,
is my greatest joy.
I hope that you can see that
joy in the last painting I did
of myself.
Please don't remember me
for the composition of my paints
or the way I used light and darkness
to capture moods,
but for being able
to read life stories beyond the
features of a face.

That's the gift I want remembered.

Shorty's Place

i was up at six thirty.
the sun was brilliant.
i made coffee and sat on the patio
overlooking the marsh
which still hadn't woken up from the winter.
the grass was a flat, dull, uninteresting brown.
the sky was clear and the crows were flying low
just above the marsh reeds and making a lot of noise.
it's a familiar place for me. i've been here many times.
the tall, ugly pine tree remains true to form.
the apple tree is starting to bloom and the bartlett tree
has flowered.
of course the willow, planted
by mr. ellis fifty years ago, was faithfully registering the
morning breeze with its thin branches.
even though it was early, two children were
riding their bikes up and down ellis road
shouting to their father who had just set free
their big, golden retriever who was happy to have the kids to chase.
a rabbit ran across the road took cover in the bush with the daffodils and myrtle.
in a deck chair, with a cup of coffee, a notepad and peace of mind,
i can't think of a better way to begin a day.

Sleet and Ramsey

yesterday morning
        before sunrise
                sleet covered the grass in the park
it was the first time
        ramsey saw icy snow
                he's from the deep south
he rolled in it on his back
        his hind legs boxed
                with the cold air
his front legs
        conducted
                a piece by leroy anderson
he smiled upsidedown
        his eyes glistened
                his tail swished
he repeated
        this same dance
                three times
once home
        he curled his shining black body
                on the mat
beside my chair
        and went to
                what we call sleep

Reflections on Montego Bay

i

the bay was rough yesterday at this time
it is smooth this morning
this makes fishing easier for the three fishermen
in their small red boat
i hope their catch is good
their lives depend upon it
the surrender of the sea
of a few fish won't make
much difference to it
but to the fishermen it will

ii

there are two golfers on the driving range
i can see them from my balcony
they are serious about taking two strokes off their game
that will make them happy
a ninety-four instead of a ninety-six
that will make them happy for a while
but they have to play again tomorrow

iii

at four thirty in the afternoon
i was trying to tell the difference
between the sound of the wind
moving through the branches
of the palm trees and the
sound of the waves washing
up on the shore

iv
when a wave reaches the shore
does it feel its job
has been done
or does it return to the sea
in search of another shore

v
it is good to be near the water
from my balcony chair i can count the colors of it
i see many shades of blue
green, gray, brown, rust
black and rose
and there is one i hadn't noticed before
      a kalamata black

Imitation Is a Compliment

yesterday just before noon
a billion and a half silver sparkles
were leaping skyward
with irrepressible repetition
from the curls of the sea's waves
trying to imitate
the dazzling brilliance of the sun above
notice the word "trying"
for if asked each spark would say
> by myself i couldn't do it
> but in company with this vast sea
> of sparks dancing bouncing leaping
> all around me- as far as one can see-
> we can put on a spectacular performance
> spectacular enough to bring the strollers on the beach to a halt
> and have them wonder
> where we learned our showmanship
> little do they know that without the sun we would be nothing
> but with it we are fascinating each of us in his or her own way
> working together with the rest to reflect the sun's brilliance
> and for a moment at least
> bringing the world to a stop
> and having it ask
>> *is there more to life*
>> *than things that can be started with a key*
>> *worn plugged into a socket*
>> *eaten or purchased and gift wrapped*
>> *or if none of these things*
> perhaps our marvelous display
> will slow them down enough
> to ask"
>> *is there something*
>> *i have forgotten*
>> *to be grateful for*
> If we can do that
> then with the sun's help
> we will have done
> what we have been
> asked to do

Field of Stones

from my balcony on the fourth floor of bushnell tower
i can look across the street to a field of thirty six stones
of different shape, size, color and age.
they were placed on a triangular piece of land
at the corner of main and gold streets
by the sculptor/artist carl andre in 1977;
he didn't want these natural
geological masterpieces to be taken for granted.
rarely do people pause to look and listen to stones.
that's a shame, for stones have
a remarkable beauty
and fascinating stories to tell.

my grandfather, part dakota indian,
told me that if i listened carefully,
stones would tell me stories,
of where they have been and
what they have heard and seen
through millions of years.

i was a kid when he told me that,
and through the busy years of my life,
when there were so many things to do,
i tucked
this important thing
in the back of my mind.
until, that is, i moved to gold street
and saw the stones
arranged neatly
just a hundred yards away
from my balcony.
then my grandfather's words came back to me.

one sunday after noon last september,
i took a walk among the stones,
their beauty unchallenged
by flowers,
as andre intended.
the stones told me that
they had all come from the
the riverbeds, fields,
and mountaintops,
of connecticut.

the river stones described their
combat with spring floods
and how they tamed their rage;
and mountain stones
delighted me with vivid tales
of eagles and hawks dancing on the wind;
and field stones told stories
of being hauled by horses to clear
open space for cattle, sheep and haying.

as i was leaving, i heard one stone say,
"come back tomorrow, we have more to say."
i accepted the invitation,
and heard about children who climb up
on them and play king of the hill,
and of lovers, who at noontime, buy hot dogs and soda
from the vendor across the street
and come back to lean up against them and
renew their promises of love,
and dirt-bikers who leap from stone to stone
without touching the ground and await the applause
of the crowd that stopped to watch.

the stones are never at a loss for words.
a big granite told me to look as well as listen.
"look at my face," it said, "it has been etched
by thousands of years of rain and snow, heat and cold.
have you ever seen a face with more
character than mine?

note the lines on my face drawn by memories
of battles being fought and young soldiers dying alone.
the smooth brownstones that border the ancient burial ground
weren't going to let this moment pass
without saying something about
the resolute settlers that put hartford on the map.
and how they'd listen to reverend thomas hooker,
the pastor of center church,
encourage his people to be steadfast
in the face of trial.

when the stones finished talking about the grit
of the city's founders,
they brought up the raucous event that happened
across the street on the night of october 27, 1687,
when captain joseph wadsworth, as the story goes,
when the candles went out,
snatched hartford's charter from under the noses
of the english emissaries who had come to rescind it,
ran down main street and stuffed it
into the trunk of an oak tree on the corner of wyllys street.

andre wants us to walk slowly when we pass the memorial
to better catch the smell of the stones after rain,
or to feel their warmth after they have baked for a day in the sun,
and to speculate about the evolutionary mysteries
they hold as they sit apparently still and silent
waiting for our imaginations to awaken.

we measure time in terms
of our passing moments.
stones don't.
they seem to be always now,
that is their gift.

The Carousel

The organ was playing loudly
and the kids were riding
brightly painted horses
with flaring nostrils and bulging eyes
going round and round
shouting at their mounts
"faster, faster!"

A tall black man
late in years
was coming from that carousel
in the park
that Sunday afternoon.

Our paths crossed
and I said,
"It brings us back to
our childhood days, doesn't it?'"

He said,
"If tomorrow I wake up with
an extra dollar
in my pocket,
perhaps I'll take another ride."
Enjoying what we said,
we parted smiling,
I toward the lily pond he toward the Arch.

Since that day,
I have thought of what he said
a hundred times,
at least.
"Another ride," to go again
with my friend Pete
as fast as we could go
to catch the rustlers
who stole cattle
from our ranch and headed
toward Wyoming's hills.

When you are ten
and the horses, white and black
are real
and can hear you when you shout
"faster, faster,"
the world is all your own.

But when the organ music
starts to fade
and the horses come to a stop
it's time to get down
take your holster and your hat
leave the carousel and park
and head for home.

The world of make believe
is left behind and you step inside again
the one they say is real,
the one in which who and whose
you really are
gets awfully confused.

If tomorrow I awake
with an extra dollar in my pocket
I'll take another ride
and retrieve the part of me I left behind

in the saddle bag of my horse called
"Sam."

nothing passes as
fast as the past does
the retirement party is over
the honors bestowed
the plaques hung
the alarm clock turned off
the agenda completed
no more meetings to attend
no more talks to give
no more trips to take
no more dinners to host
no more speeches to survive
i can put my suit in the closet
i can wear jeans
i can listen to jazz
i can read novels
i can turn off the phone
there is nothing i have to do
there is no "to-do" list
there is no schedule to follow
there is no place i have to be
there is no proposal to review
my house has been swept clean
my room is in order

it is now the kind
of place the devilish companions -
complacency indifference
laziness smugness
irritability impatience
and selfishness
like to settle down in
so i bolt the front door
i don't want them in the house
meddling with the plans
i have for the harvest
of my life
~~~~~~
"in seed time learn, in harvest teach, in winter enjoy."
William Blake, page 157 Good poems for hard times (Garrison Keillor)

The Fruit Fly

on monday morning at nine twenty,
a fruit fly landed on the altar
next to my chalice.

i watched it explore the
base of the golden mountain
looking for a foothold.

he wanted to climb
and follow the scent
of the crushed grape.

if he had made it,
what a discovery:
an ocean of wine!

i got caught up
in his exploration
and forgot the "Lamb of God".

after Mass i apologized
for the omission and
explained my distraction:

i was wondering
what this little creature's
prayer sounded like.

just then, as though on cue,
a bird on the window sill
released a loud song!

reminding us
that creatures, great and small,
have liturgies all their own.

The Man on the Corner

Trevor sits at the corner of gold and main streets.
He has been sitting on the same bench every day since 2007.
He's Jamaican- born but a citizen of this country for the last fourteen years.
As part of a walking group, I see him almost every morning at 8:30.
He is always sitting alone. I've never seen him talking to anyone.
During these cold days of winter, he wears a
 blue and gray ski jacket, thick gloves, hat with ear flaps,
 and black vinyl walking boots.
Despite the weather, he never appears to be cold.
Our daily walking routes change, but we usually end up
heading south on main. That's where we see Trevor.
He is homeless. The bench is his only home during the day.
We stopped one morning not too long ago to introduce ourselves.
He spoke to us; and seemed happy that we stopped.
Since that day, we stop and talk every morning. He likes that.
He told us that someone from the city brings him each day
a sandwich and juice. The city driver knows exactly where he'll be:
on his bench. And he makes sure that we know that it is his bench.
He says that it was "given" to him by the city;
it's near the field of immutable stones,
It was a special place, just for him.

The Moon Through My Window at 5:03

this morning at 5:03
through the large window by my desk
i saw the full moon
it was the moment
the window defined itself
in my life
without the window
facing west
i would not have seen such a sight
i stood quietly
for a while and thanked
the window for its gift
one thank you
led to another
and another
for the rain falls
snow falls
and sun falls
i reminded myself
never to let sights like these
go un-thanked
... again

The Northern Sun

caught by the glass of a tall city building,
the sun appeared to be rising in the north.
from my balcony early this morning,
i went with the illusion.
everything changed.
greenland became the "land of the rising sun",
the broadway hit was renamed
"the east side story,"
the magi saw the star and headed for india,
young men were told to "go south young man, go south,"
cowboy movies became "easterns,"
gps's had to be recalculated,
hikers kept backtracking,
adventurers found kilimanjaro in north africa,
and people stayed up late at night
to watch the eastern lights.
preposterous?
no more preposterous than
the meek will inherit the earth,
servants will become our leaders,
a coin sufficient for the taxes of
two would be found in
the mouth of a tiberian fish
and the dead will rise.

The Original Walk

The cold air has
     The morning all to itself
          There is no wind
An artist came
     During the night
          And painted the trees white
And did the same thing
     To the sidewalks
          And the frozen pond
The bells of the first church
     Across the street
          Rang seven times
As we passed
     The bronze statue
          Of Horace Wells
I said to my longtime friend
     It seems as though
     We've passed this way before
He said that we had
     Years ago
          When there was no snow

We Arrive Only To Leave

we arrive only to leave
we are never who we are
for more than a moment
then we're off in a new direction all our own
in search of whom we are becoming

each day that
we are intentionally aware
of the
people
ideas
feelings
places and events
that make up our lives
we draw closer to the original
gift of our life

people often ask where have the years gone
they have not gone
they are stored in the treasury of our lives
enjoyed
each and every time
we re-meet a friend
recall a place
revisit a feeling
re-dream a dream

that is why I feel so rich today
for my treasury
is filled with
glittering memories

it's about today
and checking
the time the sun rises
the weather forecast
the obituaries
how the senate race in connecticut is going
the unemployment rate
if the yankees won last night
how many american soldiers died in afghanistan yesterday
if the hurricane season has passed
why the fall colors are so dull this year
what movie in town is worth seeing
what caused the traffic tie-up on 84 yesterday
we are interested in all that's happening
around us
but not rightly concerned
with what's happening
in the now
of our own life
we ought to be checking
our politeness
the sound of our voice
the look on our face
our greetings
our awareness of life
our gratitude to God
the effort we put into what we do
our concern for others
our faithfulness
our morning prayer
we can get so caught up
in the daily news
that we ignore
the only
story that we've been asked
to read from beginning to end

Yellow Finch

A yellow finch
    set his feet on a branch
        of an old white oak
    tree
and looked around
    with head bobbing
        jerking and twisting
looking at everything
    the morning light
        revealed
he was where
    he wanted to be
        at that time of day on a
            branch
above the patio
    set with tables and chairs
        flowers and a
            striped umbrella
he watched me lift
    my coffee cup
        look up at him
            and speak as though
            i thought he understood
do you ever wish
    you had a fancier nest
        or a broader span of wings
            or more volume to your song
does it ever occur to you
    that you would look good
        in red or purple
        or maybe blue
or are you content
    on being who you are
        knowing that the life
            you lead comes from
                deep within

and won't allow it to be changed
    by eagles or crows
        no matter how loud they

           caw or screech
stay where you have set your feet

    upon a branch and observe
        the world and keep your thoughts your own
for a day will come
    when we may come
        to know your secrets of
           contentment
and how wrong we were
    to think the answers
        that we have
           are the only ones that are

Not Much Happened in Nazareth

Nazareth was a small town on a mountainside in Galilee.
Three hundred people lived there.
They knew one another by name.
They had similar histories of birth, school, work, and marriage.
Nazarenes stayed together.
That is the way they wanted it.
One day was very much like the others.
And so it went until the day that Gabriel came to their tiny town.

An angel in Nazareth!
Who had ever heard of such a thing?
And why had he come?
Mary a young virgin in that town got her answer.
"I have come to ask you to bear a son and not just an ordinary son but the Son of God",
Gabriel said.
If she had questions before, imagine the ones going through her mind now.
And Gabriel's explanation of how all of this was going to happen
didn't make it any easier.
He was talking for God and God's explanations
aren't ever easy to understand.

Mary's hesitation to grant the request was time's longest pause.
What if she had said "No"?
What would have happened to Nazareth?
It might have been buried by sand until an archeologist dug deep and found
the footings of a synagogue and gave Nazareth a footnote in Jewish history.
But Mary said "Yes" to the mystery.
Jesus was born and grew up to be called the Nazarene.

The little hillside town was thereafter locked in history, a fate never anticipated by
the three hundred people who picked olives and crushed grapes,
got up with the sun and went to bed with its setting.

it was evening and
andrew had just started a fire.
it was his turn to cook.
it had been a long day,
and everyone was tired.
it wasn't the best time
for Jesus to talk about leaving them,
but he had decided to get it over with.
he told them that
he was going back to the Father.
when he said that, they looked at
one another.
they had no idea
what that meant or where that was.
but they got the message:
he was leaving and leaving once and for all.
and to make things worse, Jesus told them to rejoice.
rejoice!
he had just pulled their world out from under them,
and he tells them to rejoice.

for the past couple of years, their mornings, noons and nights
had been spent with him.
as a band of faithful followers
they had walked with him up and down israel,
and heard him talk about a new kind of world
where the hungry would eat and everyone would be treated justly.
they stood only a few feet away
when he told a crippled man who hadn't
walked in years to pick up his mat and go
home to his family.

and now out of a clear night sky,
just when they were about to settle down for
a nice dinner,
andrew was a good cook-
Jesus sprang this news on them.
they lost their appetites;
they felt empty inside; it was as though
 their stomachs had been ripped out.
nothing to look forward to, nothing to live for,
no more shouting crowds asking for a king.
no more dreams of a shining kingdom.

what did they have to live for?
did he have any idea what he had just done to them?
by the look on their faces, Jesus knew they were devastated.
so he quickly added, " I leave you peace."

no one said a word. but they were all thinking the same thing.
ha! peace, what on earth is that?
we haven't the slightest idea what peace is, and that's his gift!
couldn't he think of a gift of
filling nets with fish, baskets with bread and jugs with wine?
but peace!

no one touched the lamb that andrew had cooked.
they sat in silence.
each went to bed with his own thoughts.
their thoughts worked through the night.

when morning came, they talked to one another.
"could filling our hearts with peace
be the ultimate miracle?
if we are going to live,
we have to live on that.
he filled the stomachs of thousands
with fish and bread;
certainly he can fill our lives with peace.
it's all we have to go on, so let's take
the chance.
someday, surely, we'll understand what he meant."

Proverbs

yesterday morning
i watched the sun come up
over the bay at south yarmouth.
except for two rabbits taking turns chasing each other
across the lawn of the bass river motel
and a black bird
perched on a telephone wire above me,
i was alone.
despite its predictability,
the sun's rising
is always startling.
at precisely five fifteen,
the sickle sharp red curve of the sun
inched up over the horizon and slipped
through the low clouds
and daylight began.
the vault of heaven
brightened,
the bay was paved
with pale rose light,
and a distant coast appeared.
I expected this daily recreation
to be spectacular
and i wasn't disappointed.
proverbs, today's first reading, said that the Lord had put
a lot of thought into placing mountains in their proper places,
designing a magnificent vault to frame the face of the sea,
and then filling it with a hundred billion stars.
as proverbs says, the lord wanted to delight us.

i went back to my car,
retrieved my orange and purple
styrofoam cup of dunkin donuts coffee
from its holder and took my other half of
an old fashioned donut
from a brown paper bag
and continued to reflect on
what i had just seen.
i opened the car window
and looked east again to see if anything
had changed.
it had.

the red sun had detached itself from the horizon
and hung high above it
in a perfect circle of
blazing white
so brilliant and intense that my eyes could
not stand to stare.
i had to turn away
and in my turning thought
that what i had seen before
was but a glint of
what is in store for us.
at that moment, i surrendered
my attempt at words to express
gratitude for the gift of creation
and handed my pen to the Lord.

Reaching Out

i had heard so much about Jesus
during the past year
that i had expected to see a giant
when he got out of the boat
he was tall but no goliath

the crowd surrounded him as soon
as he came up the beach
i stayed back
i listened as they called his name
i hesitated to shout Jesus
i was embarrassed
i just stood there
not knowing what to say
even if i had gotten a chance
compared to all the sick people
the really sick ones
with twisted legs and blindness and a lot of other things
i'd feel like a fool asking to be cured of the ferocious envy
i have had to live with since i was a little kid
if anyone overheard me
they'd have laughed me off the beach
but then i thought maybe i don't have to say anything to him
knowing the little i do of him
he probably can take one look at me and know the problem i am struggling with
i'll take my chances
i'll reach out and touch his robe
that might be enough
i don't need to go on and on
about how i've wasted my life thinking that everyone else
has had a better shot at life than i've had
they've got better looks more brains
magnetic personalities and money besides
so i'll sneak up on him and touch his robe
when the crowd split and i saw him coming toward me

i fell to my knees kept my face down
and my mouth shut and waited for the chance to reach out
i touched his tassel as he passed
he paused looked around then down at me
that's all it took i felt something happen in me
a strange feeling it was as though i had been flushed out cleansed
emptied and then filled up with a new life to live
and that was all i needed
to begin again

Sight for Speech Two Blind Men

Jesus asked
do you believe that i can do this

the blind men said
a strange question for a legend to ask
you walk on water
feed thousands with a word
silence screaming demons
and you ask
do we believe
Jesus touched their eyes
they closed them quickly against the light
then slowly opened them
to see what someone said was a tree

then again Jesus added unexpectedly
do not speak of this to anyone
the blind men could not believe
that he would ask them
to switch their sight for silence

on the chance they misunderstood
they followed their joy
and spent their lives in search
of the rights words to describe
the extraordinariness of the ordinary
things they saw daily

Small Seed of Faith

our table by the window
looking out over the sound
was askew.
it wobbled when the waiter
put the four vinyl menus
down beside my glass.
he apologized
for its wobbling,
bent his knee and slipped
a slim wedge of wood
beneath the culprit leg
and polished plank floor.
it didn't take much
to true the table
just a sliver of wood.
"the table of our world
is askew,"
the disciples said.
"increase our faith,
and we...
will make it right."

as though
not hearing their excuse,
Jesus said,
"the size of faith you have
is enough to move mountains
and make berry trees fly.
"attend the matters
in the corners
of your life
"and the wonders
which you wish
will appear before your eyes.

"replace your desire for vengeance
with forgiveness
and your arguing with restraint,
"purge your language of vulgarity
and cleave your tongue
to truthfulness,
"exchange your
darkened view of life
for one that's full of light.
"you need not increase
your faith
use what you have
"to adjust the
things you do
day by day
"and you'll discover
the slant of red wine
in your glass upon
"the table of your world
will flatten out.
it only takes
"an act of faith no bigger than
a tiny mustard seed
to make things right."

Sometimes It Takes Only a Few Words

sometimes only a sentence
is enough to change a life
failures multiple
giving up seems the thing to do
there is nothing else left
give up
you are beating a dead horse
forget it
you are going nowhere
try something else
then someone you have known for a long time
a friend with whom you have shared life
says
>   you'd be a fool to quit
>   you like what you are doing
>   keep doing it
that's all it takes
nothing spectacular
just a simple sentence
and boldness returns
you start re-thinking ideas
re-tracing your steps
soon the failures are forgotten

and you begin thinking
this time success
the spirit revives
it leaps
a new life begins
never fault the power
of words
to make good things restart
elizabeth had a lot of troubling things
going on in her life
as the final days of her labor drew near
simple things were getting harder to do
the pains in her back
worsened

she dreaded the things
she once liked doing
then something happened
a young girl came up the hill
to her home and greeted her
with a few words
and the baby leaped in her womb
she knew immediately that things would be all right
that's all that it took
a few words
and their sound was enough
to make her young again
anxious to see what life held
in the life she held within

A Stubbed Toe

stubbing a big toe
is a common human experience
who hasn't banged the large one
against the leg of a cabinet
while trying to navigate
a darkened room
in the middle of the night
on our way to wherever we
were going
the pain is memorable
and the resolve to turn on the
light the next time resolute
we learn from experience
...at least some of the time
stubbing a toe is nothing
compared to the mistakes
we make in daily living
trying to navigate
in the dark
just think of the times we've
gotten up in the morning and cursed
the foolish mistakes we've made
the night before
because we let anger get the best of us
or the doubts we have about
the life we've been living
rather than deciding
to make the best of
each new day given
or giving up on prayer
because events didn't go the
way we wanted them to go

it is never easy when things like this happen
but the life and words of Jesus
help us to keep them in perspective and
his promise of being close
always gives us strength
with Jesus at our side
we'll find our way even
through a furniture store at midnight
that is why today
Jesus calls himself
the light of the world

The Beatitudes

thousands of people
walked to Mount Tabor
from all parts of Palestine
to see and hear Jesus

when he came down from
the mountain
and stood on the plain beneath
the crowd surrounded him

it was the moment
they had come for
a chance to be near the one
who could hear and help them

soon they thought
there would be food
 and freedom for all
and no more sickness no more pain
Jesus looked intently at the people
and spoke poetically in
rhythms of contrasts and contradictions
as the prophets and psalmists before him did

the poor will inherit kingdoms
the hungry will be well fed
the sorrowful will laugh long and loud
and the shunned will be embraced

as he spoke
tears of joy flowed from the eyes of the crippled
and children danced in circles
having been given a chance to dream
Jesus paused and looked at his new disciples
a mixture of shepherds and money changers
mystics and sinners
rulers and those never called by name

He told them he saw joy in their eyes
and heard it in their voices
but joy is vain
he said
until it is shared with others

these words shocked them
in a sentence
he told them that his work
was now theirs

on the way back to their homes
 one of the new disciples said
if i heard him right he said that we will be happy
only when we see joy in the eyes and hear it in the voices
of all people no matter who they are

do you think we'll ever get to see that day
another disciple
who had come up from behind him
said simply
Yes

The Flock Woven Like a Web

his flock is a web
movement anywhere
    ripples everywhere
when a lamb strays
    he feels it
he leaves to find it
    hidden by a hill or tangled in a bush
he listens for its bleat
    and follows it
when a shepherd loves his sheep
    trust pushes his steps
opens his eyes
    and sharpens his ears
the web quivers again
    he knows the lamb is near
he has but to reach out
    and lift it to himself
back to his pasture
    he walks to the center of the fold
and places the lamb with the rest
    and immediately the web grows still

The Planned Stoning

the woman accused of adultery crouched down
in the circle drawn in the sand
for her execution.
she wrapped her arms around her head
as a shield against the pain about to begin.
she knew what was in store for her.
when young she had to watch other women
die by stoning.
it was part of her education.

the courtyard of the temple
was the usual scene for this
kind of spectacle.
 the large crowd
that gathered
 was always noisy;
stoning of this sort was a spectator sport.
the young and the old shouted
with every direct hit to the head;
whose stone would do her in?
whose throw would be the
final signature of justice?

then suddenly the crowd went quiet.
those who thought that
they knew the mind of God
confronted Jesus and asked
what he thought of this.
Jesus bent down to draw in the sand.
But that wasn't what they were looking for.
they wanted words; would he throw a stone at her
in obedience to the law of Moses, yes or no?
if not they could condemn him, too.
Jesus stood up straight, looked them in the eye
and said," let the one among you who is without sin
cast the first stone."

again he bent down and began writing in the sand.
with each written word another of the accusers turned
and walked away.
 the crowd left, too.
when all were gone,
Jesus helped the woman to her feet and looking
her in the eye said, "is there no one to condemn you?"
"no,"
"nor do I. go and sin no more."
the woman turned and stepped
out of the circle,
paused and looked back at Jesus.
 he had set her free. no longer was it about her past
 but about the future he had just
given her.
inspired by the look in his eyes
and the sound of his words,
like so many before her,
she confidently walked out of the temple courtyard
and began living the rest of her life.

Friends and Forgiveness

That Aaron was paralyzed didn't stop his friends;
they carried him on his stretcher wherever they went.
When they heard that Jesus was at a home in their town,
they carried Aaron to him for healing.

The crowd around the house was huge; they couldn't get in,
but young and bold, they climbed to the roof top,
spread the slats apart and lowered Aaron's stretcher
down to the feet of Jesus.

Looking at the friends of Aaron
Jesus said, "As for you, your sins are forgiven."

They were caught off guard.
They had come to have Jesus free Aaron from his stretcher
 so that he could walk with them to the trout streams,
but discovered that they were the ones set free.

They hadn't anticipated that their love for Aaron
would change their lives in ways
they could never have imagined.

Upside Down

there are some temptations i don't find hard to resist
a plate of raw oysters blood pudding and boiled cow's tongue
are among them
but putting words into the mouths of gospel characters
is a temptation i can't let pass untaken today
i give into the temptation to have peter interrupt Jesus and say
what do you mean follow me
haven't i been right behind you for the past three years
with the exception of the climb to the top of calvary
for which i am terribly sorry and won't ever forget
i've been on your heels all the way

yes I know that you've been following me
Jesus said
but from now on it's going to be
harder for you to match my steps
 I'll be gone
and you'll be in my sandals
you'll feel the stripes
feel the thorns
feel the lance
and finally
your whole world will be turned upside down

Walk with Me

walk with me.
where?
wherever i go.
we'll hike the paths to small towns.
we'll walk the plains of jericho.
we'll climb the mount of tabor.
we'll travel the highway to jerusalem.

i will ask you to ascend the heavens
past rainbows and over clouds.

i will ask you to traverse the surface of the seas
seeking distant lands,

i will ask you to go to
people everywhere
and tell them
that what they know
is but the beginning of what
they'll someday know.

What Did Jesus Just Say

several years ago
a little girl asked me
if Jesus ever spoke to me
i said
yes
when
she asked
just now
i said

have you heard Jesus speak to you
i mean directly to you
or have other people told you
what he said to you
there is a huge difference between
what Jesus says to you
and what people say he says
to you

today Jesus is speaking in
the temple court yard and it is
packed with people who have
come miles to hear him
they want to hear him for themselves
and not rely on hearsay

he is poised
self confident
he knows what he wants to say
and he says it loud and clear
the audience is fascinated by him
it is as though he is speaking
to each one of them personally

they hang on his every word
each word is a revelation
it opens their minds and hearts
to a new way of looking at
the world
it gives them hope

it's no wonder that
when the priests and scribes
tried to rile up the crowd
to kill him
they were ignored

the crowd was hanging on
every word that Jesus spoke
they would treasure them
carry them with them wherever they went
live and die with them

when Jesus
speaks directly to you
his words come back to you
like echoes from
a mountain top
time and time again
at the oddest moments
and in the strangest places

listen to him carefully
and you'll get an idea
why the people in the courtyard
didn't pay a bit of attention
to the call for his death

Your Words Are Spirit and Life

are we listening
when his voice asks us to
learn the language of bees
pay attention to those we once thought wrong
walk a path we thought too rugged
write in verse
draw in ink
hear from inside out
hear what dogs say when we leave the house
hear what dawn says when it first breaks across the sea
hear what fields say when they go dry
accept the invitation of stars to wonder what's beyond
record the stories of stones
appreciate the dance of leaves
stoke the fires of imagination
say what once you thought bizarre
dive from a higher platform
anguish over the waste of words
seek the right words
eliminate the wrong ones
wonder why pigeons sit in rows
ask why people argue in public places
and guess what birds are
singing about at seven twenty four in the morning

Why Are You Weeping

Jesus was the reason Mary got up in the morning
went about her day happily
knowing that he cared where she was
what she was doing
once he had come into her broken life
everything changed
the sounds of the earth spoke
where once they made only noises
the colors of the earth were eyes' gifts
where once they only defined space
the clouds and trees danced
where once they only moved
the tomb was empty
her soul was empty
the excitement was gone
her joy could not be shared
nor could his
that was why she was crying

Breaking of the Bread

the disciples usually followed Jesus
but today is different, he follows them.
two disciples are leaving Jerusalem for their home in Emmaus.
Jesus catches up with them.
they don't recognize him.
he asks what they are talking about.

"are you the only one in Jerusalem
who doesn't know what happened to Jesus,
our people's hope; how he was seized and crucified
and buried in a tomb which three days later
was found empty by some women
who were told by angels that he had risen?"

Jesus asked them,
"did you not know that this was how it was to be?"
he went on to speak of many things

prophets and saints
sinners and kings
and spoke as though it was written from within
and not something he had heard in school.
his companions listened to everything he said
but failed to recognize his voice or face.
he was as much a mystery to them then
as he was when first he called them to follow his footsteps
 no matter where they went.

the journey to Emmaus was about to end.
Jesus didn't stop.
it appeared that he was about to go on.
they said stay with us for the day's end is near.

a table was set
a meal prepared.
Jesus took a piece of bread
broke it in two and it was in the breaking
that they knew that he was the people's hope.

at dawn, the disciples hurried back to Jerusalem
to tell the others that Jesus had risen from the tomb
and that in the breaking of the bread
their beating hearts
told them what their minds had missed

The Andes from My Window

from my window early this morning
i looked down on the night's
heavy snowfall
it covered the piles of snow
that had already been pushed
onto the median
and the curbs by the plows
which had worked all night
i thought that i was looking down on
the andes from the moon
and I wondered what
the angels thought when they
saw the first snowfall on planet earth
then I wondered
if Jesus ever saw snow in the Judean hills
if he did
he never mentioned it

The Withered Hand

I was born with
    A shriveled hand
        An outcast
            Shunned always and everywhere
People say that sometime
    Along the line
        My father sinned
            And I owe for it now
Even in this place of prayer
    I stand in the back
        Out of the way
            In the shadows
Where no one can see me
    Hidden and quiet
        Alone and ashamed
            With my withered right hand
But the preacher
    With the eyes of a teacher
        Paused and
            Saw through the dark
Come out of the darkness
    Come into the light
        Take your place with me
            Up here in front
And then he continued
    Stretch out you hand
        So that all here
            Can see
That your past
    Is undone
        And your
            New life's begun

And the dreams
        You had locked
                In your head
                        Are set free
Two miracles occur
        In moments like these
                One is of me
                        The other of you
What you do with your
Life from now on
        Rests in your hands
                So begin it and it will be

The Call of Simon and Andrew

the sea defined peter and andrew
    they were fishermen
they made a living
    catching and selling fish
their spirits rose and fell with the sea's
    stingy and generous moods
rejoicing when their nets were full
    sullen when they weren't
at dawn they headed for shore
    and if the sea were kind
they emptied their nets
    and headed for the marketplace
but this dawn their routine
    changed dramatically
a stranger interrupted
    their folding of nets
and asked them
    to follow him
to leave the sea they had grown up with
    to walk with him whom they had never met
there have been times in our history
    when pauses seemed interminable
but not this time
    the answer
spoken by their feet
    came immediately
they entrusted their lives
    to him
on nothing more than
    the sound of his voice
peter and andrew looked back
    their nets had been washed away

A Small Man Packed with Passion

paul was a small man packed with passion
at dawn he was breathing murderous threats
against the followers of the Lord
at sunset he was
proclaiming the Lord's name
and all this within the markers of a day

on his early ride to Damascus
for persecution's sake
he was toppled
from his horse by a blinding sky light
his companions led him
to the city by hand
once in Damascus the hands of another man
opened his eyes to his next passion-
preaching

the lord is always on the lookout
for people of passion
for they are the ones
who destroy or serve

as always the lord
took the chance
as he did with all those he called
that paul
would spend his passion
on service not destruction

Jesus Explained in Private

after Jesus told the parable of the mustard seed
to the crowd
he took the disciples aside privately
to explain it

the disciples had questions
Jesus had answers
Matthew had a pen and paper
and wrote everything down
      are all the birds of the sky
          doves and hawks
              crows and nightingales alike
        welcome to
      settle in the branches
Jesus said
      yes
then
      are any ever asked to leave
Jesus said simply
      No
what we wouldn't give
for a copy of Matthew's notes
today

He Had Nothing to Say

the full moon at
        midnight accompanied by mars
the wind that soothed his
        face in the burning sun
the touch of a hand
        while walking through the woods
he had nothing to say

birds flying in triangles
        above his head at dawn
children running and
        dancing in the street
taste of red wine
        and ripe figs
he had nothing to say

river water
        rushing by his feet
tears that flowed
        not knowing why
rain bouncing
        off dusty roadways
harp strings
        touched by old fingers
he had nothing to say

nothing that is until
        his friends begged
a man named Jesus
        to loosen his tongue
and open his ears
        then the words came
and feelings flowed
        and those who loved him
stood by
        and wondered why
they had missed so much

The First Heron of Spring

just before seven this morning
i saw a grey heron in the park pond
it's the first one I've seen this spring
chances are it had just returned
from wherever it had spent the winter
he likes it here-
  the sounds of buses and cars bending around
the curves of jewell street
the colored blinking traffic lights
on the corner of trumbull and wells streets
the dogs that stop to stare at his
spindly legs
and long sharp nose
and wonder how he can stand so long
motionless
  until his moment comes
to do what he came to do
and then the noisy flight up and over the trees
spreading his wings wider than
the reach of an oak tree
past the gleam of the capitol dome
and the angels Gabriel and Raphael
on the towers of the arch
he is happy to be back in Hartford
I can tell
this is his kind of place
he chose it over the ponds
deep in the woods
he likes
the city's noise
  the hustle
  the people's differences
he can be himself here
after all he is a different kind of bird
soon his mate will join him

and together they'll enjoy -
the carousel music
the shouts of kids
the ball games on the lawns
the lunch time walks of office workers
and even the ducks
with paddling feet
ah- the city where there is always something happening
he loves it here
and I suspect
he wishes it would be ever spring

The Barber Shop (Part I: Insincerity)

the man in the barber chair next to me
on Holy Thursday morning
was giving his opinions
on Hartford to the barber
in a voice loud enough to cover the
the hum of the clippers
i could hear him easily
he bet the barber
that the new twenty-four hour
subway shop on maple avenue
would be shot up by
a gang before the end of the month
having finished with the south end
he went to the north end
and said that if the barber really wanted
to learn how to hate black people
he'd have to live next to them
for three years...as he had
when the barber finished
the man got up
paid and tipped him
and said offhandedly
Happy Easter

The Barber Shop (Part II: Sincerity)

on easter morning at six thirty
i walked ramsey through the park
it was a misty foggy morning
he doesn't mind that kind of weather
sitting next to the carousel
was a man
in his late forties
he might have spent
 the night on a park bench
at his feet was a blue duffel bag
stuffed with `crumpled clothes
when we got near to him
he said
what a beautiful dog
what's his name
ramsey
can i pet him
sure he loves it
then ramsey nuzzled closer to the man's breakfast
a bag of potato chips
the man smiled broadly
and said honestly
Happy Easter

The Barber Shop (Part III: Mystery)

the wind blows where it will
and you can hear the sound it makes
but you do not know
where it comes from or where
it goes
so it is with everyone
who is born of the spirit
obviously it bypassed the
barber chair
but not the park bench

A Short Story of Love

as i was passing a hackberry tree
in the park
late last september
i thought that i heard it talking

i stopped to listen
sure enough
i heard the old warty trunk
talking
he asked its pointy leaves
if they could be anything they wanted
to be in the future
what would they wish to be
they said
that they'd like to be pages
in a note pad so that children
could write the stories
they and their many toys
talked about in the middle of the night
when everyone but they in the house
were fast asleep

the trunk thanked the leaves
for their thoughtfulness
then turned to the branches
and asked
the same question
we'd like to be drum sticks
they said
in the hands of magical musicians
that will beat to a rhythm that
everyone in the world
knows is out there somewhere
but has yet to be heard

i sensed that the trunk was delighted
by the image the branches drew
then he looked at the
huge shadow that stretched from his roots
to the edge of the duck pond

the shadow anticipated what was coming
and answered
that it would like to be a tranquil dream
that didn't obey the rules
of night and day
and couldn't be picked up
and stolen by thieves
and claimed as their own

after a short silence
the others together
asked the trunk
what his plan for the future was
i wish to be a comfortable bench
he said
on which people could sit and let
their gracious feelings flow
like hillside brooks
into a meadow pond
and spill over endlessly onto
 all people animals and earthly things

before returning home
i stood alone
and watched the ducks
draw arrowheads on the quiet
surface of their pond

Susanna and the Elders

the elders' lust didn't boil over
at the sound of the garden gate,
it had been heating up for years.
and for all we know,
it boiled over many times in the past,
but they got away with it
trusting the axiom-
if we can we will.

the big difference, however,
between this day in the garden
and past episodes elsewhere,
is Daniel; he wasn't around when
they pulled rank before.

Daniel was born wise.
he knew a lecher when he met one
...or two.
and these elders might have gotten away with
this dastardly scheme if they knew
their trees.

if they had spent more time in the park
studying the trees they would have known
the difference between a small mastic shrub
and a tall warty oak.

the last bit of wisdom Daniel was heard
giving the elders as they prepared to get their severance pay
was, "if you had introduced yourself to
the 100,000 different species of trees in the forest
you wouldn't have had any time left over for lusting."

Rose Garden: There Comes a Time

yesterday we walked through
the rose garden in elizabeth park
the roses weren't out
    it's too early
the thorned bushes
    were ready for them
        but they'd have to wait
so do we

beyond the garden
    there was a plot
        filled with tulip plants
waiting to bloom
they too had to wait
or at least we thought so
until we turned to leave
and saw on the far side of the plot
          a red and yellow tulip standing alone
            it had refused to wait
its time had come
    to come alive
        and call for us
          to walk to its side
and say for it to hear
    you defined your time
        didn't you
          and didn't wait
    did you

Two Thousand Pigs in the Sea

what a sight it was
two thousand pigs
in the sea of galilee
once the people Gerado
got over the economic impact
this would have on the herders
merchants and householders
they realized how much the freedom of one man
possessed by the
demon named legion
meant to the man named Jesus

The Delicacy of the Moment

each moment is a gift
enter it
hold it
be to it
give to it
take from it

you are not alone in it
angels are in it
sun and moon are in it
wind and rain are in it
birds and animals are in it
ocean waves are in it

living is in it
breathing is in it
seeing is in it
hearing is in it
feeling is in it

sounds are in it
sights are in it
promises are in it
joys are in it
disappointments are in it

sadness is in it
hope is in it
failure is in it
renewal is in it

miracles are in it
healings are in it
beginnings are in it
endings are in it

meetings are in it
leavings are in it
winnings are in it
defeats are in it

moments are delicate
treat them carefully
they only come
to us
for so long
so don't ignore them

Scurrying

every once in a while
 a word in a gospel catches my attention
today it is scurrying
i like it because it is a vivid word
i can picture the people of gennesaret
  hurrying from town to town
  and house to house frantically
  looking for the sick and crippled
  putting them on mats
  and carrying them as fast as they could
  back to the side of Jesus
they wanted their friends to be cured
  and Jesus was the one to do it.

i can identify with the hurried pace
there are days when i don't think
  there is enough time to do the things
  that need to be done
scurrying is the word i think of
go here get there it's late
there's no time to spend
  detailing for Jesus what i need
time enough is all i have
 to reach out and touch his robe
and according to the gospel today
  that's all it will take to get my strength back
slow down and do what i have to do
i thank mark for
  choosing the word scurrying
  it hit just the right note for me
  and often that's all it takes
  the right word

Who Do You Say I Am?

in a museum
we stand back to look
at a masterpiece to better appreciate
the genius of the artist
from a distance we get a different perspective
on his or her intent
the same rule is advised
when looking at Jesus
our perspective is different
now than when we first began
following him seriously
when young i would have been
able to answer his question
with a blue book definition
today i can't for Jesus is not a definition
for me he is an experience
with each reflection on his life i am inspired
to imitate his mission of bringing light to dark places
hope to those who have given up on life
courage to those who feel they have nothing more to give
in answer to his question this morning
i couldn't have answered as quickly as peter
i would have said simply "Jesus"
hoping that he'd understand
that he is the sum of all that has happened to me
since we first met

The Greatest Temptation

i am alone in the desert
    far from home
    thinking of my youth
and of my days on the shore of Galilee
    watching the evening sun sneak
    into the sea
and of afternoons
    in the mountains
    listening to brooks
and their peculiar sounds
    rolling over and around
    ancient stones
and days
    of summer wishing to have
    the rain fall hard upon my face
knowing what a small delight
    that was compared
    to earth's gratitude
and of nights
    hearing the sound
        of waves against the boat's bow
while waiting
    with my father for the catch
    that would make our time together
in darkness
    so worthwhile
    and of the noisy grind of the pulley
hoisting a bucket of water
    to the well's brim
    and the appeal the water's slosh
made to quench
    my dry throat at day's end
    and then suggesting
that I take time
    to stand on the shore
    now

at sun's breaking and watch
        the sea quiver at the wind's touch
and of the last drips of rain as they fell from
        the sycamore branches
        onto the back yard flowers
and the time when it fell heavily upon the road's dust
        and had it erupt into a million
        small volcanoes
and how it unleashed bursts of laughter
        from young boys and girls who
        ran along
the shore's edge in just enough tide to cover
        their toes and splash the legs of those
        running beside them
and of the wonder that filled me as i watched
        it fall from heaven with one drop
        seemingly just like another
yet different enough to change earth's seeds
        into wheat and lilies
        and olive trees
        alone
        in this enormous
        desert silence
these and other
        thoughts like them
        I hold tightly
for they're all from
        the path I've taken
        which has led me here
and now you Satan
        are attempting to tempt
        me with power fame and wealth
but these
        are not the things
        that entice me
if you really wish to tempt me
        you will lead me to a mountain top
        and lay before me

all the joys I knew
      before I stepped into the Jordan River
         and stepped out into the crowd
the crowd that grows day by day
      and wants more of me
         than I can give
I might be tempted
      to step back into the river
         and return to Nazareth
but no you do not
      understand me and
      you never will...will you

Three Brief Reflections on Cana

Part One

Jesus changed water
into- wine
to show the wedding guests
that they too can perform miracles
by shielding the ones they love
from embarrassment

Part Two

the wedding feast went dry
a man they hardly knew
changed six jugs of water
into wine
done not for power's proof
but simply out of kindness

Part Three

when Jesus came to Cana
the second time
a young man and woman
were the first to recognize him
as the wedding guest
who changed water into wine
and humiliation into happiness

Naaman the Leper

Naaman doesn't fit the mold of a leper
when he rings a bell
it isn't to warn people that he's coming
it's to have his servant bring breakfast
when he approaches a city's gate
it isn't for food but for rampage
he lives in the palace of the king
holds the rank of general
and the servant girl who brings him coffee
is one of the spoils of victory
and it is this servant that tells him that
his leprosy can be cured by a prophet
she had heard of in her homeland
listen to her the kings says
and sends him on his way
 in Israel Naaman meets the prophet Elisha
who tells him to go and wash
in the Jordan river seven times

Naaman scoffs
i could have done the same thing back home
in one of my own rivers
and come out just as clean
but again his servant's wisdom prevails
he plunges into the river
and after the seventh plunge
he comes up as clean as an angel's wish

when Jesus tells the Nazarenes
that a foreign leper would
listen to the word of god before they do
they try to throw him off a cliff...so much for tolerance

Psalm 96 Keeps Us Busy

if you did what
psalm ninety-six,
asks you to do,
you'd be busy all day.
it asks you to get up
at four thirty
and welcome the day's
first light with a new song,
not one that you've heard before,
but a new one that you've
composed especially
for the occasion,
preferably a lively one
to catch the attention
of a still sleepy world.
furthermore, it can't be a re-hash
of what the world has already heard.
startling, stunning, and smart
is what it calls for; something that
would make broadway producers
envious.
just as every day is
a new creation, so ought our song be.
God would like to hear
something original
and as though that is not enough,
the song must be an endless burst
of melodic praise in honor of god's name.
keeping in mind that
God's name has been praised
by musical geniuses for centuries,
to say nothing of the
angelic choruses which have done
an outstanding job over the last span of eternity.
once this is done
we must end with
some solemn
Beethovian tones to convey
 our gratitude for salvation.

Lost in a Dark Place

both Ezekiel and the psalmist use images
of darkness to accentuate the
feelings associated with being lost.

Ezekiel's sheep
have wandered off and had gotten lost
in the low, dark clouds weighing heavy
on the hillside.

they couldn't be seen by the shepherd.
he called. he heard their bleat
and entered the low clouds
and found them frightened
huddled near a berry tree.

and the psalmist identifies himself
as a sheep walking through a
dark valley but despite the darkness
remains calm for he knows the shepherd
is close by, protecting him.

the message today
rests on these images of darkness
as periods of life.

there are times when we lose our way.
things get muddled and
 our confidence collapses.
but the shepherd is unrelenting
in his search for us.

he listens for our call
and descends into the darkest valley
when he hears our voice.

the darkness opened by the lance
on Calvary remains open,
it never closes,
for those lost but
wishing to be found.

The Quaking Aspen Trees

in the evening,
beneath the Quaking Aspen trees,
     that ridged the banks of the Euphrates,
the Judean captives, accompanied by the harp,
sang songs of their homeland:
the olive groves and vineyards on the hillsides,
the refreshing streams and verdant pastures,
the laughter in the city square and sunlight on the temple.

under the golden leaves of the Aspen shimmering in the western sun
they prayed that their tongues would cleave
to the roofs of their mouths and their hands grow numb
if they forgot to sing of the glories of Jerusalem.
for song kept their hopes alive for the day
when they'd turn their backs
on the earthly allure
of Babylon
with its palaces, wide streets, schools of science,
sky high towers honoring Marduk, their god,
lush gardens and market places filled with satins and silks,
and freely head home for the land given them by God.

Trust Jesus

Through the Fox Memorial entrance from Wells Street
into Bushnell Park
between a tall Bald Cypress tree and a Ginkgo tree
there's a green trash barrel
with a poster pasted to it
telling everyone in big red letters to
Trust Jesus.
It's seen by hundreds of people each day.
What they trust Jesus to do
is anyone's guess.
Some trust Jesus
to convince them that his
time has no definition;
that making a difference in life
has nothing to do with age;
that wondering what is beyond the farthest star
is a great blessing,
and that the final word on any subject
has yet to be spoken so they're to keep searching
for it even if they have to make it up.

And finally there are some who take
the banner on the barrel
as a commandment to get rid
of the trash in their lives and trust
that Jesus will replace arrogance with meekness,
stinginess with generosity,
and foulness with decency.

Here's a situation where the pastor is a poster
and the pulpit is a barrel.

Time to Say Good-Bye

Jesus had been with his disciples for three years.
They had gotten used to having him around.
Their days began and ended in his company.
When they were
hungry, he fed them
thirsty, he gave them drink
tired, he led them to restful waters
sick, he healed them.
When they returned from a journey,
he was there to
       listen to their stories,
       dispel their doubts,
       praise their efforts,
       mend their torn hopes.
He was everything to them.
There wasn't a thing he couldn't do.
And even though they were responsible
men and women,
they became dependent upon him.
They couldn't imagine life without him.
They chose not to think of life without him.
He was everything they ever dreamed of,
a man who knew what he was about
and determined to reach every goal he set for himself.
But now, he says,
"it is time to say 'good-bye'."
I am going back to the Father.
You will be on your own from now on
but I know that you can do it.
I was watching you
when you thought I wasn't
and saw how the crowds took to you so easily knowing
that you were in this for them
and not for yourselves;
I heard how kindly you talked to the poor and listened
to them up to the end of their stories,
and watched how the children came to you
sensing that their words meant as much to you
as those of the rich and powerful.

Don't be afraid
I won't leave you alone.
While out of the world's sight,
I will be at your side every step of the way,
to remind you that you are me in your time
and without you I cannot be.
So walk on bravely now
and when your journey's done
you will say,
'we did it... yes, with you,
but it was we who did it .'

The Lord's Voice

the lord's voice
roars above the waters
the lord's voice
stirs the water's depths
the lord's voice
pushes the clouds
the lord's voice
splits the skies
the lord's voice
rattles on roof tops
the lord's voice
lifts the wings of birds
the lord's voice
bends the palm trees
the lord's voice
leaps among the bougainvillea
the lord's voice
wakes those who sleep
the lord's voice
opens closed eyes
the lord's voice
loosens clogged ears
the lord's voice
invites the mute to speak
the lord's voice
beckons all to follow
the lord's voice
summons all to lead
the lord's voice
announces the dawn
the lord's voice
asks the sun to shine
the lord's voice
proclaims the universe
the lord's voice
reveals the beauty of creation
the lord's voice
says "Arise"
the lord's voice says "Live, another day is here"